# 20TH CENTURY SCIENCE AND TECHNOLOGY

# 1920-40

## ATOMS TO AUTOMATION

Please visit our web site at: www.garethstevens.com
For a free color catalog describing Gareth Stevens' list of high-quality books
and multimedia programs, call 1-800-542-2595 (USA) or 1-800-461-9120 (Canada).
Gareth Stevens Publishing's Fax: (414) 332-3567.

Library of Congress Cataloging-in-Publication Data

Parker, Steve.
    1920-40: atoms to automation / by Steve Parker. — North American ed.
        p. cm. — (20th century science and technology)
    Includes bibliographical references and index.
    ISBN 0-8368-2943-3 (lib. bdg.)
    1. Science—History—20th century—Juvenile literature.  2. Technology—
History—20th century—Juvenile literature.  [1. Science—History—20th century.
2. Technology—History—20th century.  3. Technological innovations.
4. Inventions—History—20th century.]  I. Title.
Q125.P3252    2001
509.042—dc21                                            2001020781

This North American edition first published in 2001 by
**Gareth Stevens Publishing**
A World Almanac Education Group Company
330 West Olive Street, Suite 100
Milwaukee, WI  53212  USA

Original edition © 2000 by David West Children's Books.  First published in Great Britain
in 2000 by Heinemann Library, Halley Court, Jordan Hill, Oxford OX2 8EJ, a division of Reed
Educational and Professional Publishing Limited.  This U.S. edition © 2001 by  Gareth Stevens, Inc.
Additional end matter © 2001 by Gareth Stevens, Inc.

Designers: Jenny Skelly and Aarti Parmar
Editor: James Pickering
Picture Research: Brooks Krikler Research

Gareth Stevens Editor: Dorothy L. Gibbs

Photo Credits:
Abbreviations:  (t) top, (m) middle, (b) bottom, (l) left, (r) right

AKG London:  pages 4-5, 17(b), 19(b).
Corbis:  pages 4, 5(t), 6(b), 8(l), 15(m), 20(m), 21(br), 22(b), 24(bl, br), 25(both), 26(b),
    26-27(b), 28(b), 28-29(t), 29(b).
Corbis Digital Stock:  page 7(t).
Hulton Getty Collection:  cover (br), pages 8(t), 12(b), 12-13, 13(b), 14(both), 15(t, b),
    16(both), 16-17, 18(both), 19(t), 21(bl), 24(t).
Jodrell Bank Service Centre:  pages 6-7.
The Kobal Collection, Hulton Getty Collection:  cover (m).
Mary Evans Picture Library:  pages 20-21, 23, 26(m), 26-27(t), 27(b).
Science & Society:  pages 28-29(m).
Vitra Design Museum:  pages 5(b), 22(t).

Printed in the United States of America

1 2 3 4 5 6 7 8 9 05 04 03 02 01

# 20TH CENTURY SCIENCE AND TECHNOLOGY

# 1920-40

## ATOMS TO AUTOMATION

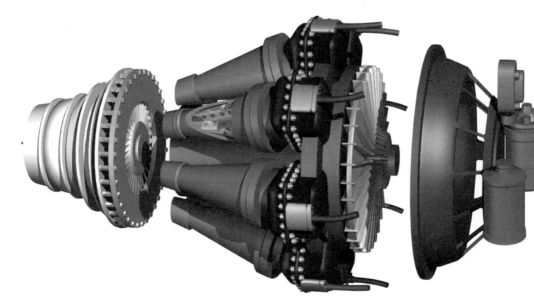

## Steve Parker

Gareth Stevens Publishing
A WORLD ALMANAC EDUCATION GROUP COMPANY

# CONTENTS

*In 1928, Spanish engineer Juan de la Cierva (1895–1936) piloted the autogiro he invented in 1923 across the English Channel.*

*The race to build skyscrapers, such as New York City's Empire State Building, led to new construction techniques — and new dangers.*

# SCIENCE AND POWER

During the 1920s, people in developed countries began to feel the benefits of technology and science. Factories, offices, and even ordinary homes were wired for electricity, and improvements in mass production affected almost every area of daily life. Clothing, furniture, and all kinds of labor-saving gadgets, as well as buildings and vehicles, became better — yet more affordable. By the 1930s, new and improved models of cars and trucks crowded newly surfaced roads. For longer distances, millions rode in comfort on speedy new railroads. People with more money, or less time, could use passenger airlines. With radio already well established, the new electronic wonder was television. In science, researchers attempted to unravel the secrets of the Universe, probing both tiny atomic particles and vast galaxies. Optimism was in the air. Toward the end of the 1930s, however, the world was again at war. The same science that had promoted prosperity and peace now turned to creating weapons powerful enough to destroy Earth itself.

*"Nude" stockings were among the new types of clothing that came with the development of nylon and other synthetic fibers.*

*Lighter, stronger metals and plastics were molded and shaped to make slimmer, more graceful products.*

# DEEP SPACE

**The discovery of radio waves coming from far-off stars and galaxies and of Pluto, the smallest and most distant planet, showed how tiny Earth really is.**

## RADIO ASTRONOMY

In 1931, when American radio engineer Karl Jansky (1905–1950) was studying shortwave radio sources, such as lightning bolts, that cause static and interference, he noticed some weak radio waves that seemed to come from the sky, rather than from Earth. More experiments showed these waves came from outer space — from the center of Earth's own galaxy, the Milky Way. In 1932, Jansky suggested that stars and galaxies send out radio and other types of waves, as well as light waves, all of which are forms of electromagnetic energy. Jansky's discovery was the beginning of radio astronomy, a science that has told us a lot about the origin and possible fate of the Universe.

*Karl Jansky's work led to huge radio telescope dishes like this one in the United Kingdom at Jodrell Bank, Cheshire. Radio telescopes detect invisible waves, such as microwaves and radio waves, coming from objects in space.*

*At Bell Telephone Laboratories in New Jersey, U. S. engineer Karl Jansky was trying to identify sources of interference in telephone communication when he discovered radio waves coming from space.*

6

U. S. astronomer Clyde Tombaugh (1906–1997) discovered Pluto in March 1930. This dark, icy ball of rock is the smallest planet in Earth's solar system. It is also the planet farthest from the Sun.

## HOW SMALL WE ARE!

In the 1920s, U. S. astronomer Edwin Hubble (1889–1953) discovered that Earth's galaxy, the Milky Way, was only one of thousands. Working at Mount Wilson's Lowell Observatory in Arizona, Hubble identified wispy objects deep in space, which were thought to be clouds of gas, as other galaxies. He also noticed that, even when taking into account the effect known as "red shift," light coming from farther galaxies was redder than it should be, which meant the farthest galaxies were moving away from each other the fastest. This phenomenon was excellent evidence to support the Big Bang theory.

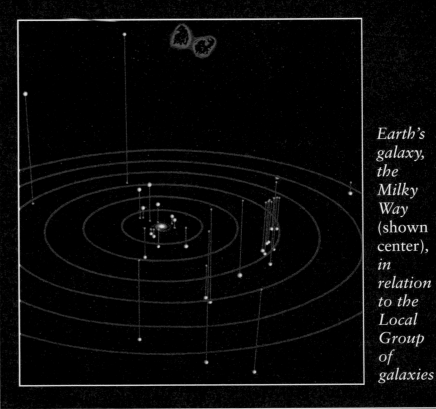

Earth's galaxy, the Milky Way (shown center), in relation to the Local Group of galaxies

# HOW IT ALL BEGAN

As cosmologists developed the work of Edwin Hubble, the incredible vastness of the Universe became clear. At the same time, fossil hunters were digging up the past to uncover the amazing antiquity of humankind.

*Hubble's look at space through the Palomar Schmidt telescope in 1949 was a look back in time.*

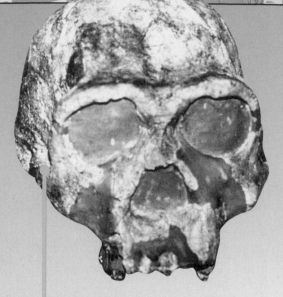

*A fossilized skull in South Africa pushed back human evolution millions of years.*

## SEEING STARS

During the 1930s, the many astronomers who followed up on Hubble's work saw evidence of millions of galaxies along with other mysterious objects in deep space. Some of these star clusters were so distant that light coming from them took billions of years to reach Earth. Consequently, we see these distant objects as they appeared billions of years ago. Looking into deep space is almost like looking back in time.

## THE BIG BANG

In 1927, Belgian astronomer Georges Lemaître (1895–1966) proposed the idea that all matter in the Universe was once contained in a single, gigantic, "primal atom." Lemaître's idea has grown into the modern Big Bang theory. A huge explosion of the atom, some 12 to 15 billion years ago, caused the Universe to expand, and, according to this theory, the Universe is still expanding. The work of Lemaître and other pioneer space scientists during the 1920s and 1930s continues to be developed and debated today.

2. *After a few hundredths of a second, the Universe expanded to the size of the Sun.*

3. *For a million years, the Universe expanded and cooled, forming atoms of hydrogen and helium.*

1. *The Big Bang*

## A MISSING LINK?

In 1925, a small fossil skull found in South Africa shook the world. Known as the "Taung Child," the skull was studied by anthropologist and surgeon Raymond Dart (1893–1988), who named the creature *Australopithecus africanus*.

Dart decided that the creature lived some two to three million years ago and was something between prehistoric apes and the humans of today — an "ape-child." Supporters of the theory that humans have evolved from apes said the Taung Child skull was evolution's "missing link." Today, many experts believe that, although this creature might not have been a direct ancestor of modern humans, it was a member of the human family that had died out or become extinct.

*The temperature at the edge of the Universe remains at about 1,800 billion° Fahrenheit (1,000 billion° Celsius).*

*The outer region of space is some 10,800°F (6,000°C), which is about as hot as the surface of the Sun.*

*Normal space is about -450°F (-270°C).*

*4. As the Universe continued to expand, other elements formed.*

*5. The Universe is still expanding and might continue to expand forever, or it might eventually reverse — and collapse.*

9

# WORLD SCIENCE

During the 1930s, particle physics was a growing area of scientific research. Advances in high-powered electrical devices produced so-called atom-smashing machines capable of breaking atoms into pieces. Atom smashing, in turn, led to the creation of new substances and chemical elements for scientists to test.

## NEW ELEMENTS FROM OLD

Atom smashers, such as cyclotrons, used electrical and magnetic energy to move atomic particles faster and faster through long tubes. When the particles reached incredible speeds, they were aimed at targets, such as metals, and smashed the targets' atoms to pieces. Many new particles were discovered this way, including, in 1932, the positron, which is a positive version of the electron and the first known "antimatter."

## THE PERIODIC TABLE

The periodic table is a chart of all known chemical elements. It arranges the elements by atomic number into horizontal rows, or periods, and vertical columns, or groups. The elements in a group have properties similar to each other but are increasingly heavy. The atomic number is the number of protons in the nucleus of one atom of the element.

## A SMASHING TIME

American physicist Ernest Lawrence (1901–1958) invented the cyclotron in 1931. Inside a cyclotron, particles travel along a spiral path between the poles of a powerful electro-magnet. Rapidly reversing pulses of electricity create a changing magnetic field that gives the particles more and more speed. Lawrence received the Nobel prize for physics in 1939. Element 103 is named after him.

**Periodic table:**

period 1
| H 1 |
|---|
| Hydrogen 1 |

period 2
| Li 3 | Be 4 |
|---|---|
| Lithium 7 | Beryllium 9 |

period 3
| Na 11 | Mg 12 |
|---|---|
| Sodium 23 | Magnesium 24 |

period 4
| K 19 | Ca 20 | Sc 21 |
|---|---|---|
| Potassium 39 | Calcium 40 | Scandium 45 |

period 5
| Rb 37 | Sr 38 | Y 39 |
|---|---|---|
| Rubidium 85 | Strontium 88 | Yttrium 89 |

period 6
| Cs 55 | Ba 56 | La 57 |
|---|---|---|
| Cesium 133 | Barium 137 | Lanthanum 139 |

period 7
| Fr 87 | Ra 88 | Ac 89 |
|---|---|---|
| Francium 223 | Radium 226 | Actinium 227 |

| Ti 22 | V 23 | Cr 24 | Mn 25 |
|---|---|---|---|
| Titanium 48 | Vanadium 51 | Chromium 52 | Manganese 55 |
| Zr 40 | Nb 41 | Mo 42 | Tc 43 |
| Zirconium 91 | Niobium 93 | Molybdenum 96 | Technetium 98 |
| Hf 72 | Ta 73 | W 74 | Re 75 |
| Hafnium 178 | Tantalum 181 | Tungsten 184 | Rhenium 186 |
| Rf 104 | Ha 105 | Sg 106 | |
| Rutherfordium 261 | Hahnium 262 | Seaborgium 263 | |

**Lanthanides**
| Ce 58 | Pr 59 | Nd 60 | Pm 61 | Sm 62 | Eu 63 | Gd 64 | Tb 65 |
|---|---|---|---|---|---|---|---|
| Cerium 140 | Praseodymiun 141 | Neodymium 144 | Promethium 145 | Samarium 150 | Europium 152 | Gadolinium 157 | Terbium 159 |

**Actinides**
| Th 90 | Pa 91 | U 92 | Np 93 | Pu 94 | Am 95 | Cm 96 | Bk 97 |
|---|---|---|---|---|---|---|---|
| Thorium 232 | Protactinium 231 | Uranium 238 | Neptunium 237 | Plutonium 244 | Americium 243 | Curium 247 | Berkelium 247 |

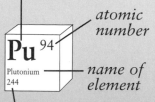

*chemical symbol*
*atomic number*

| Pu 94 |
|---|
| Plutonium 244 |

*name of element*

*atomic mass (the number of protons and neutrons in one atom)*

## GAPS IN THE TABLE

The periodic table was developed in 1871, but the table had some gaps. Scientists believed there were elements to fill the gaps, but these elements either did not exist on Earth or were too rare on Earth to detect.

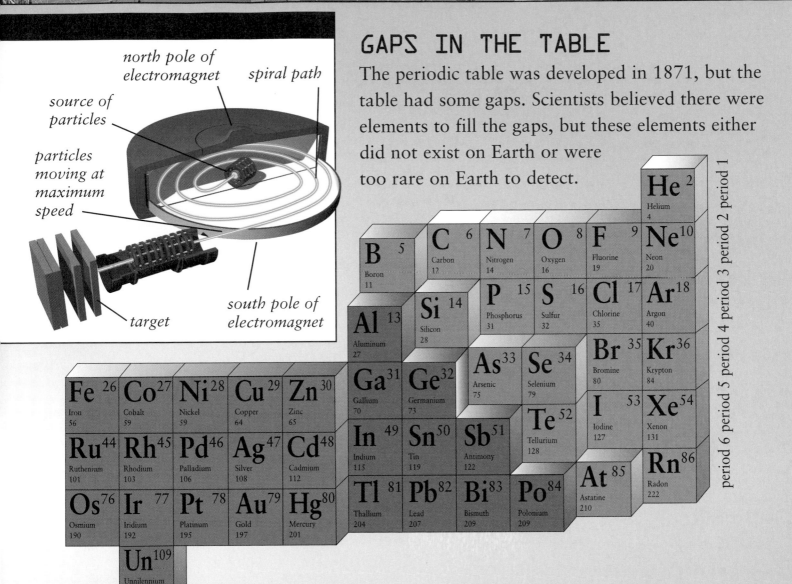

north pole of electromagnet

spiral path

source of particles

particles moving at maximum speed

south pole of electromagnet

target

period 1 · period 2 · period 3 · period 4 · period 5 · period 6

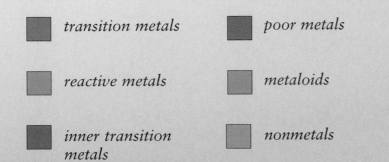

transition metals

reactive metals

inner transition metals

poor metals

metaloids

nonmetals

## FILLING A GAP

In 1937, Emilio Segrè (1905–1989), an Italian-American chemist, neatly filled the gap in the periodic table for element 43. The new element was named technetium (Tc). Segrè used an atom-smashing cyclotron to bombard element 42, molybdenum, with particles called deuterons, which are nuclei of deuterium, a hydrogen isotope known as heavy hydrogen. Isotopes are atoms of the same element that have different weights, or atomic masses. The element hydrogen has a total of three isotopes.

# FASTER AND BIGGER

At the cutting edge of technology during the 1930s were new ways to go faster and to make things look bigger. By 1938, the liquid-fuel rocket, first launched in 1926, had been greatly improved, and a powerful new engine, the jet, was introduced. With another new invention, the electron microscope, life-forms too small to be seen with a light microscope became visible.

## ROCKET MEN

Solid-fuel rockets, such as fireworks, had existed since ancient times, but American engineer Robert Goddard made a liquid-fuel rocket that could fly in the airless vacuum of space. His first launch was in 1926. By 1938, Wernher von Braun (1912–1977), in Germany, was building larger, faster rockets.

*Robert Goddard (1882–1945), the world's first successful rocket scientist (far left), supervises work on a liquid-fuel rocket built in 1940. Goddard's experiments between 1909 and 1945 led to the development of space-age rockets, missles, and satellites.*

12

combustion chamber

fuel inlet

exhaust nozzle

compressor fan

### THE WHITTLE JET ENGINE

A jet engine sucks in air, compresses it with fans, and sprays fuel into it. The fuel burns in a continuous explosion, and extremely hot gases roar out of the exhaust nozzle in a fierce stream — the "jet." The force of the gases blasting backward thrusts the jet engine forward. One of Whittle's main challenges was developing materials that could withstand the heat of the explosion.

## JET POWER

A jet engine is similar to a rocket, but it does not carry its own oxygen supply to burn fuel, so it cannot fly in airless space. British engineer Frank Whittle (1907–1996) thought about making a jet as early as 1928, while he was still a student. Whittle fired up his first working jet in 1937.

*Whittle (right), in 1948, with one of his jets*

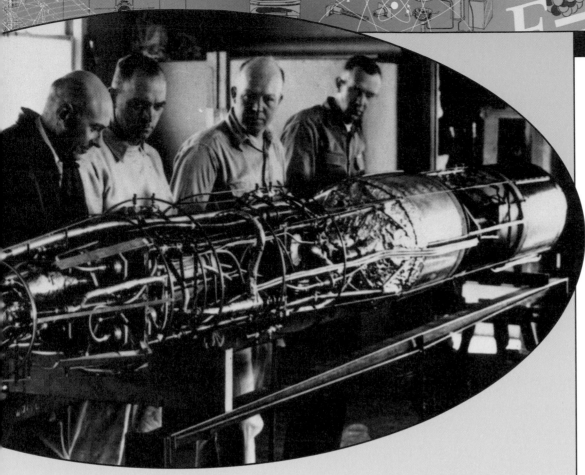

Robert Goddard's 1926 rocket was the first liquid-fuel rocket to fly. The way it operated established the basic principle for all liquid-fuel rockets today. Because rockets fly in airless space, both fuel and an oxidant must be carried on board. High-pressure gas pushes the fuel and the oxidant into the combustion chamber, where they are ignited to provide thrust.

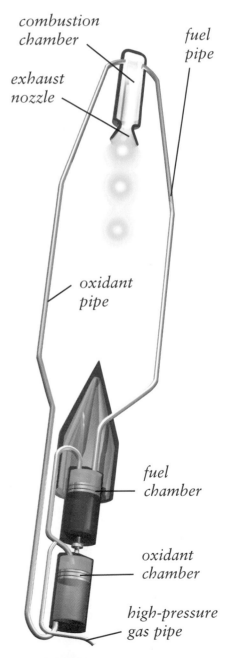

combustion chamber

fuel pipe

exhaust nozzle

oxidant pipe

fuel chamber

oxidant chamber

high-pressure gas pipe

13

*By 1950, electron microscopes magnified 70,000 times. They were used to study the tiniest life-forms — viruses.*

## THE BIGGEST OF THE SMALLEST

An ordinary microscope uses light waves to magnify tiny objects such as body cells and bacteria, but the length of a light wave limits the magnification to about 2,000 times. In 1931, Ernst Ruska (1906–1988), a German physicist, built a microscope that, instead of light waves, used electron beams, like those in a television set. In 1933, he improved it to magnify 12,000 times, enabling biologists to see the smallest types of germs.

# ON THE MOVE

When production of the Model T Ford, the first mass-produced automobile, ceased in 1927, more than 15 million of them had been built. In the 1930s, a new wave of popular cars took to the roads, and the roads themselves were improved to handle the increasing number and speeds.

*Percy Shaw (1890–1976) invented the cat's eye reflective road stud in 1934.*

## PEOPLE CARS

One of the Model T's great successors was the German KdF-Wagen, designed by Ferdinand Porsche (1875–1951), which went into mass production around 1938. This automobile was later renamed Volkswagen (VW), or "People's Car." It offered many technical improvements, such as torsion bar suspension and an air-cooled engine that reduced the weight, expense, and risk of freezing that were characteristic of a water-cooled engine system with a radiator.

*Because the first mass-produced Volkswagens had a shape similar to a beetle, they came to be called "Beetles."*

14

## A SHINING INVENTION

British inventor Percy Shaw got the idea to create the "cat's eye" road stud when he was driving in fog and saw the reflection of a real cat's eyes in his car's headlights. It has been said that the cat's shining eyes made him stop just in time to avoid driving over a cliff! The cat's eye road stud is a block of glass set into a base with a special casing to protect it from the weight of traffic. The block's many sides are angled to reflect light rays back in the same direction from which they entered. Modern cat's eyes are self-wiping and come in different colors for different road positions.

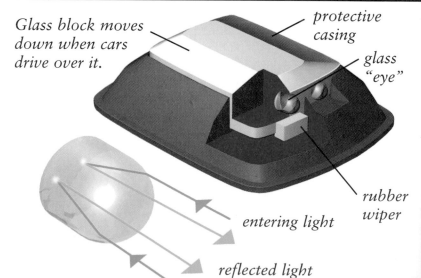

*Glass block moves down when cars drive over it.*

*protective casing*

*glass "eye"*

*rubber wiper*

*entering light*

*reflected light*

## BETTER ROADS

Besides new surfaces, the whole idea of roads and highways changed. Germany was the first country to think of highways as places for fast, safe, comfortable, long-distance car travel, without slow traffic turning in from small side streets. In 1921, Germany opened an autobahn, the first wide, straight road that could be recognized as a modern highway or expressway.

*With the onset of World War II, German leaders saw the value of VWs for military use, so the government financed their production.*

## ROAD SURFACES

As vehicles improved, roads had to improve, too. The loose stones on roads suitable for horse traffic were thrown up by car tires. New road surfaces were developed using sand, gravel, and crushed stone mixed with asphalt and cement.

*The first long tunnel for cars was the 1.6-mile (2.6-kilometer) Holland Tunnel between New York City and New Jersey, which opened in 1927.*

*One of the first two-lane highways opened near Munich, Germany, in the early 1930s.*

# CROWDED SKIES

One of the goals for long-distance travel was to cross the Atlantic Ocean from North America to Europe. In 1927, a determined airmail pilot amazed the world with his solo flight from New York to Paris.

## "LONE EAGLE"

*For his historic flight, Lindbergh piloted a Ryan M2 aircraft nicknamed the Spirit of St. Louis.*

Although other pilots had crossed the Atlantic before him, Charles Lindbergh (1902–1974) was the first to complete a nonstop flight — alone. Lindbergh left New York on May 20, 1927, and flew to Paris, a distance of more than 3,600 miles (5,790 km), in 33 hours, 29 minutes.

*Approaching the mooring mast at Lakehurst, New Jersey, the Hindenburg turned into a horrific fireball.*

## ROTOR WINGS

After World War I, many engineers tested aircraft with wings that whirled around like the blades of a fan. These rotor wings created lift even when the aircraft was not moving forward, enabling it to hover. The first practical helicopter, the Focke-Wulf Fw-61, flew in Germany, in 1936, at a speed of about 75 miles (121 km) per hour.

*A central engine on this 1923 experimental helicopter turned four rotors. The rotors were arranged in a square for stability.*

aluminum
alloy frame

hydrogen
cells

tail fin

engine

passenger
area

control room

At 812 feet (247 meters), the *Hindenburg* was the longest airship ever built. It was three and a half times longer than a Boeing 747 jumbo jet and could carry more than 70 passengers. Its hydrogen gas was contained in 16 separate, baglike cells.

## END OF AN ERA

The first regular passenger flights across the Atlantic were on airships, many of them built by the Zeppelin Airship Building Company. These sky monsters were held aloft by lighter-than-air but flammable hydrogen gas. The *Graf Zeppelin* first crossed the Atlantic in 1929 with 20 passengers. Its sister ship, the *Hindenburg*, built in 1936, made frequent transatlantic trips. On May 6, 1937, while docking in the United States, the *Hindenburg* burst into flames, killing 36 people. This disaster ended the airship era.

17

In 1923, Juan de la Cierva had an idea for a new type of aircraft, the autogiro. Like an airplane, it had a front propeller that was powered by an engine. It also had a rotor on top. As the craft gained speed, the rotor whirled around naturally in the airstream to provide additional lift.

# RAILROAD FEVER

In the 1930s, railroads were under a lot of pressure to improve. Air travel, although more expensive, was much faster. Trucks carried bulk cargo. People enjoyed the freedom of having their own cars and not being tied to stations and schedules. Railroads fought back with bigger, faster locomotives and more luxurious passenger cars.

## INTERURBANS

From about 1900, especially in the United States, many cities and large towns were connected by interurbans, which were local railways with trolley-like passenger cars powered by electric motors. Interurbans were much like the commuter railroads around some large cities today. For most people, however, automobiles were much more convenient. By mid-century, most interurbans had faded into disrepair.

## STEAM VERSUS DIESEL

As the size and power of diesel engines increased, they challenged traditional steam locomotives. Diesels were generally quieter, caused less sooty pollution, and did not have to stop as often for water and fuel.

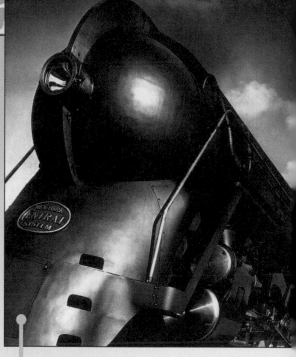

*The American Locomotive Company introduced Hudson steam locomotives in the early 1930s. By that time, engineers knew the importance of streamlining for high-speed travel.*

*In July 1938, the British Mallard set the rail speed record for steam locomotives at 125.5 miles (202 km) per hour. This record still stands.*

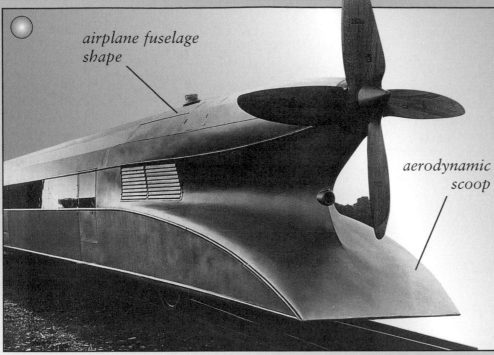

airplane fuselage shape

aerodynamic scoop

## THE "PLANE-TRAIN"

Railroad technologists tried many new ways to achieve greater speed and efficiency. The *Railway Zeppelin* was an experimental locomotive, built in Germany and tested in 1931. It combined various design and engineering features from airships, propeller aircraft, and other locomotives, and it did away with pistons, as well as with connecting rods and other wheel-turning machinery. A scoop at the front allowed the propeller to push air backward, rather than blow it against a normally blunt nose.

## THE RISE OF THE RAILCAR

When diesel locomotives first took to the rails in 1924, a passenger car called the diesel-electric railcar soon became popular around cities. With a diesel engine to power electric motors for the wheels, it did not need long, expensive power lines like the electric interurbans.

*The diesel-electric* Flying Hamburger *was named for the route it traveled between Berlin and Hamburg, Germany. In 1933, it was the first high-speed railcar in regular service.*

# TESTING METALS

During the 1920s and 1930s, some of the greatest manufacturing advancements resulted from the development of new materials. Steel and other metal alloys, plastics, and artificial fibers gave industrial engineers a new range of design possibilities.

## THE GOLDEN GATEWAY

One of the most spectacular examples of a use for the new steel alloy was the Golden Gate Bridge over the entrance to San Francisco Bay in California. The delicate beauty of this bridge made it world-famous. Although the project began in 1933, the bridge did not open until 1937, due to problems with the foundations for its 745-foot (227-m) steel towers. One of the towers had to be set into a huge concrete block built in a cofferdam on the ocean floor. The span between the towers of this magnificent bridge is 4,200 feet (1,280 m). The suspension cables are 37 inches (93 centimeters) wide.

*Steelworkers had to set up a catwalk (above) before installing the two main suspension cables on the Golden Gate Bridge (top).*

## REINFORCED CONCRETE

Although reinforced concrete was first developed in about 1850, it was not widely used until the invention of the elevator and the growth of skyscrapers in the 1920s. Reinforced concrete is made by pouring liquid concrete into a mold that has a framework of thin steel rods. The concrete hardens, forming a strong, flexible material ideal for building tall structures of almost any shape.

*1. A network of steel rods is placed inside a form, or mold.*

*2. Liquid concrete is poured into the mold.*

*3. The mold is removed after the concrete hardens.*

To make steel strips, beams, and girders, molten, or melted, steel can be cast in a solid block or an ingot and then squeezed between massive rollers until it is cold. This hot strip, or continuous casting, method was devised in about 1923. The steel is pushed through many sets of rollers while it is incredibly hot and semiliquid to produce long, strong strips.

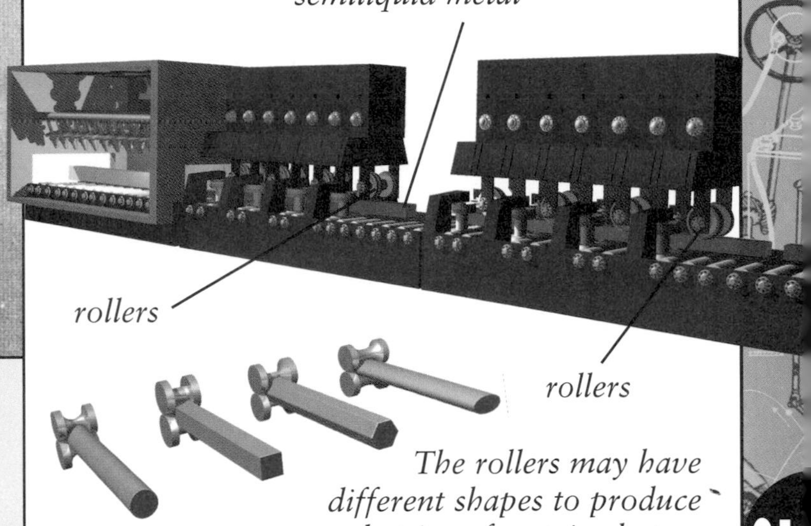

*semiliquid metal*

*rollers*

*rollers*

*The rollers may have different shapes to produce metal strips of certain shapes.*

21

## GOING UP

Built with hot strip steel beams and girders, skyscrapers really got going in the 1930s. At 1,050 feet (320 m), New York City's Chrysler Building was the tallest in 1930. In 1931, the Empire State Building set the record at 1,250 feet (381 m).

## FAST-TRACK BUILDING

The Empire State Building did not employ particularly new construction techniques, but it was built amazingly fast — in only 1 year, 46 days. Materials were delivered daily, and as the framework for upper floors was being bolted and riveted, lower floors were already being finished.

*In November 1930, the Empire State Building was a steel "skeleton" (right), but it was completed (left) by April 1931.*

# MODERN MATERIALS

The materials revolution of the 1930s quickly spread from industry to the home. Technologists produced all kinds of strong, lightweight substances, including steel and aluminum alloys, Bakelite and other plastics, and artificial fibers, such as nylon and rayon. These materials could be molded and shaped, giving product designers more freedom than ever before.

## FROM BICYCLES TO ARMCHAIRS

The new materials encouraged slimmer, more graceful shapes for cars, furniture, and home appliances. In 1925, Hungarian designer Marcel Breuer (1902–1981) started a "modernist" trend in design by adapting the construction of his tubular-steel bicycle frame to make armchairs and other furniture.

*The Landi chair, designed in 1938, was made of aluminum and could be left outside in the rain.*

## MAKING ALUMINUM

The shiny, silvery metal aluminum is so useful because it is light and does not rust like iron or steel. It is, however, quite brittle, so it is often combined with other substances to form tougher alloys. Pure aluminum is produced in large pots, or cells, using a process called electrolysis. In this process, a strong electrical current is passed through a mixture of cryolite and anhydrous alumina, which is obtained from bauxite, the main aluminum ore.

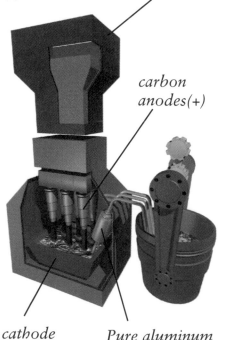

*Molten alumina and cryolite are poured into a hopper.*

*carbon anodes(+)*

*cathode floor(-)*

*Pure aluminum is pumped out.*

## NYLON'S CHEMISTRY

Raw nylon is a hot liquid that is spun into fibers. American chemist Wallace Carothers (1896–1937) produced it by heating hexamethylenediamine with adipic acid at a temperature of 518°F (270°C). Besides being a superior fabric, nylon's smooth hardness also had industrial uses.

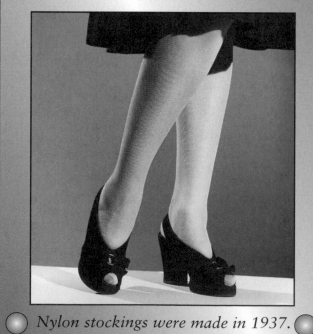

*Nylon stockings were made in 1937.*

22

## SYNTHETIC SILK

For centuries, people had used only natural fibers, such as cotton, wool, and silk. Then, in about 1884, chemists began to experiment with an artificial, machine-made fiber produced from cellulose found in plant matter such as wood pulp. By 1892, production methods had gradually improved to the viscose process, creating a fiber called rayon that could be made into a fabric very similar to silk. The first rayon garments were stockings, produced in Germany in 1910. In the early 1920s, the first mass-produced rayon clothing offered the look and feel of silk at only about one-fifth the cost.

## OTHER NEW FIBERS

Synthetic fibers took another leap forward with the invention of nylon in 1934 by Wallace Carothers. Just two years earlier, in 1932, Carothers had produced the first successful artificial rubber, called neoprene. By 1937, strong, smooth, mass-produced nylon was an instant hit with garment makers. Sheer nylon hosiery, or stockings, became known simply as "nylons."

*Traditionally, stockings were made of cotton or wool and covered the legs and feet to keep them warm. In 1924, stockings made of rayon were a daring new fashion. With sheer, light rayon, legs looked bare!*

## MAKING ARTIFICIAL FIBERS

Nylon, terylene, and other artificial fibers are usually made in chemical laboratories. They are known as polymers. Cellulose is a natural polymer from plant-based matter such as refined wood pulp. It was used in the 1870s and 1880s to make the first versions of rayon. In about 1923, breakthrough technology permitted the mass production of rayon from cellulose sheets.

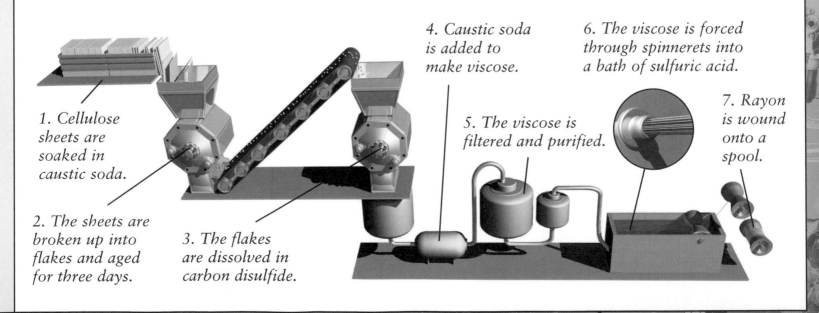

*4. Caustic soda is added to make viscose.*

*6. The viscose is forced through spinnerets into a bath of sulfuric acid.*

*1. Cellulose sheets are soaked in caustic soda.*

*5. The viscose is filtered and purified.*

*7. Rayon is wound onto a spool.*

*2. The sheets are broken up into flakes and aged for three days.*

*3. The flakes are dissolved in carbon disulfide.*

# MASS MEDIA

By 1920, many homes and offices were equipped with a variety of electrical devices. In the following years, technology seemed to focus on improving them. Some became safer, more reliable, more stylish, or smaller. Others made the world smaller!

## AM/FM

The mass medium of the age was radio. Regular broadcasts began in the United States in 1920, and, within a few years, most homes had a radio set. At first, all systems were amplitude modulation (AM), in which radio waves vary in amplitude, or height, to carry the coded information for sounds. Frequency modulation (FM), in which waves vary in frequency, or number per second, came in 1933.

*Electric typewriters date back to 1901 and became suitable for popular use by the 1920s. This model is from 1925.*

24

*This 1930s radio has both AM and FM tuning bands. FM gives a clearer sound but has a more limited range.*

## MASS PANIC

The power of radio was evident in 1938 when American actor and director Orson Welles (1915–1985) broadcast his dramatized version of H. G. Wells's novel *The War of the Worlds.* Believing that Martians really were invading Earth, thousands of people rushed into the streets in panic.

*Many people thought Orson Welles's account of Martian aliens attacking Earth was a true news broadcast.*

## THE FIRST TV

The first regular public television broadcasts using the all-electronic system we have today were in 1936, in England. More than ten years earlier, Scottish engineer John Logie Baird (1888–1946) had invented a partially mechanical system with a fast-spinning disk. The British Broadcasting Corporation used Baird's system for its transmissions from 1929 to 1936.

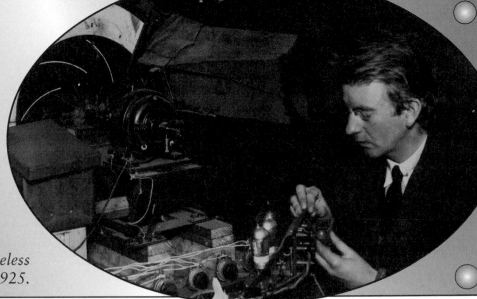

*Baird experimented with "wireless vision" TV equipment in 1925.*

*In 1939, TV was a scientific wonder despite a television receiver's small screen and blurred picture.*

## LIGHT – CAMERA – TELEVISION

Since the 1870s, television has developed in stages. In the 1920s, Russian-American physicist Vladimir Zworykin (1889–1982) made a screen that contained many photoelectric cells, each producing an electrical current related to the brightness of light falling on it. Zworykin also developed a screen with tiny dots that glowed when hit by cathode rays, which are actually electron beams. Zworykin's two pieces of equipment became the television camera and the TV set.

## INSIDE A TV SET

Inside a television, a high-voltage electron gun gives off cathode rays. Electricity passing through a focus-scan coil bends the rays and makes them scan across the screen in a line, then another line below it, another line below that, and so on. As electrons hit the screen, they make the tiny dots that cover the screen glow, forming the picture.

*electron gun*

*focus-scan coil*

*screen*

*cathode ray*

# DISEASE CONTROL

In 1928, at St. Mary's Hospital in London, Scottish doctor and microscope expert Alexander Fleming (1881–1955) made one of the greatest of all medical discoveries.

## PENICILLIN

Fleming noticed that a small, round dish in which he grew bacteria and other microbes seemed to have been contaminated by a green mold, or fungus, that must have floated through the air and landed on the dish. As the mold grew, it destroyed the bacteria that were supposed to be growing there. Fleming guessed that the mold produced an antibiotic, or "anti-life," substance that killed the bacteria. The mold was identified as the genus *Penicillium,* so Fleming called the antibiotic substance "penicillin."

26

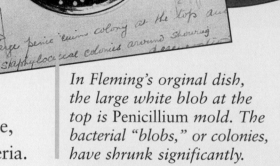

*In Fleming's orginal dish, the large white blob at the top is* Penicillium *mold. The bacterial "blobs," or colonies, have shrunk significantly.*

## A LIFESAVER

Initial tests showed that penicillin barely harmed people, yet it killed many harmful bacteria. It was extremely difficult, however, to purify large quantities of the substance so it could be studied properly. In the late 1930s, Australian disease expert Howard Florey (1898–1968) and German-British biochemist Ernst Chain (1906–1979) overcame these difficulties. During World War II, penicillin was used to treat wound infections, saving countless lives.

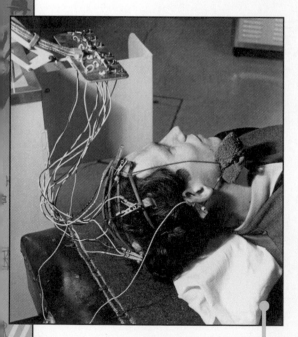

*The electroencephalograph (EEG), which detects tiny electrical signals from the brain, was developed in 1929.*

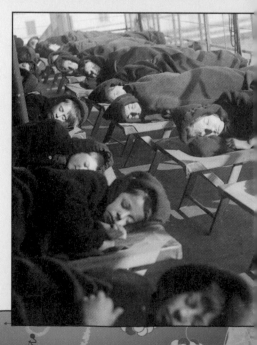

*In 1945, Alexander Fleming received the Nobel Prize in Physiology or Medicine jointly with Florey and Chain.*

Diabetes is a disease usually caused by a lack of insulin, a natural hormone that controls blood sugar. In 1921, at the University of Toronto, Canadian doctor Frederick Banting (1891–1941) and his assistant Charles Best (1899–1978) prepared a pure, active form of insulin and saved a dog with diabetes. Insulin treatments have since saved millions of human lives.

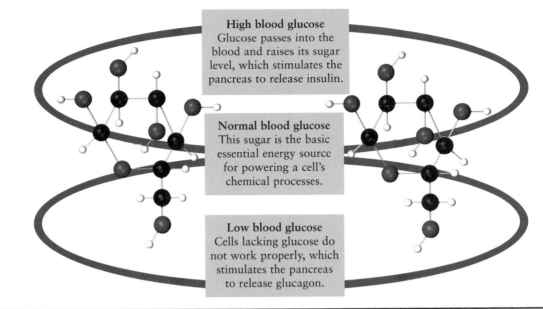

**High blood glucose**
Glucose passes into the blood and raises its sugar level, which stimulates the pancreas to release insulin.

**Normal blood glucose**
This sugar is the basic essential energy source for powering a cell's chemical processes.

**Low blood glucose**
Cells lacking glucose do not work properly, which stimulates the pancreas to release glucagon.

# THE FIGHT AGAINST MALARIA

Each year, the disease malaria affects hundreds of millions of people and causes more than a million deaths. Malaria is an infection of tiny, one-celled parasites called *Plasmodia* in the red blood cells of humans bitten by *Anopheles* mosquitoes. When DDT was discovered in 1939, hopes rose in the battle against malaria, but, in the 1950s and 1960s, DDT was found to be very harmful, and its use is now strictly controlled.

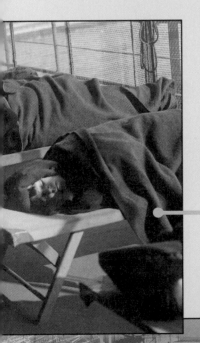

*In 1923, the Bacillus Calmette-Guérin (BCG) vaccine was developed to fight the terrible disease tuberculosis (TB).*

## THE BAD AIR DISEASE

For centuries, malaria was thought to be caused by stale or putrid air. *Mal aira* means "bad air." In 1897, mosquitoes were found to be the real carriers. Swiss chemist Paul Müller (1899–1965) produced the insecticide DDT to control many kinds of flying pests, including mosquitoes. Müller received a Nobel prize in 1948. He could not have foreseen DDT's harmful effects.

*Only female mosquitoes spread malaria. The males do not suck blood.*

# GADGETS GALORE

A complete list of the labor-saving gadgets and appliances developed during the 1930s and 1940s would fill this book. Many of them have faded away, either because they were never really useful or because they have been replaced by updated versions. Try to imagine life, however, without ballpoint pens and sliced bread.

WARNER BROS.
Supreme Triumph

AL JOLSON
*in*
The JAZZ SINGER

*The Jazz Singer was a silent movie with music and speech added later, using phonograph records linked to the film projector.*

## "YOU AIN'T HEARD NOTHING YET"

These words came from singing star Al Jolson in the 1927 "part talkie" movie *The Jazz Singer*. The first full-length movie with sound was *Lights of New York* in 1928.

### "THE BEST THING. . .

. . .since sliced bread" is one way to praise a new invention. In 1930, sliced bread itself was a new invention. Although it saved only the few seconds it took to find a knife and cut a slice of bread from a loaf, it was popular from the first day. The electric carving knife arrived in 1939. Fortunately, Band-Aids had been introduced in 1921.

*Sliced bread was one of the first convenience foods.*

*By 1920, electric toasters had been around for some time, but the 1932 Magnet boasted extra-fast toasting.*

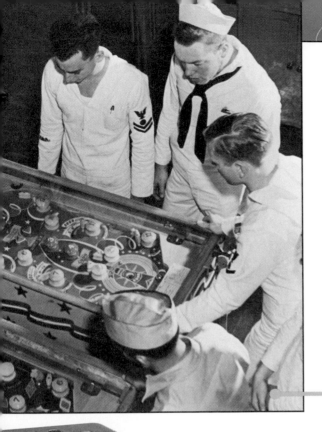

*Pinball machines and jukeboxes were invented in the 1930s. They filled some of the leisure time created by all the new labor-saving gadgets.*

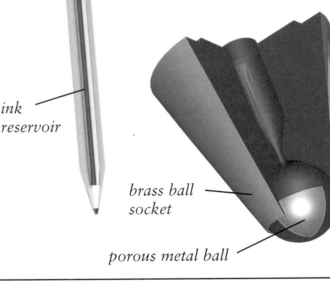

pen barrel

Hungarian-born inventor Lazlo Biró patented the ballpoint pen in 1938. It was intended for use by aircraft crews while flying at high altitudes, where low air pressure caused fountain pens to flood or blob. Ballpoint pens, often known simply as "biros," first went on sale in Argentina in the early 1940s. An improved version, the Reynolds model, came out in 1945.

ink reservoir

brass ball socket

porous metal ball

**29**

## LEISURE TIME

Factories were automated. Travel by car was faster than waiting for a bus or a train. Homes were full of gadgets that saved time and effort. Precooked, frozen convenience foods by Birds Eye went on sale in 1939. All of these changes meant people had more time, so inventors created and manufacturers produced new devices to fill it.

Radios, televisions, and phonographs became very popular, as did cruising through the countryside in the family car. When the first tape recorders went on sale in Germany, people could store their own voices, sounds, and music. It seemed as if science and technology had an answer for everything.

*Electric razors appeared in 1931. This picture was taken with X rays, which were also fairly new.*

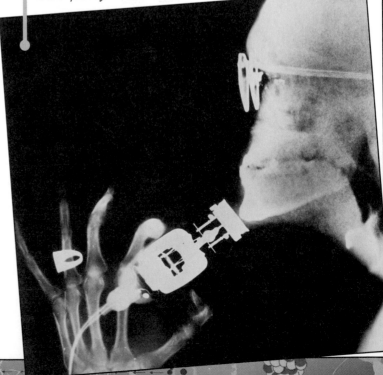

# TIME LINE

| | WORLD EVENTS | SCIENCE EVENTS | TECHNOLOGY | FAMOUS SCIENTISTS | INVENTIONS |
|---|---|---|---|---|---|
| **1920** | •U.S.: women get vote | •Michelson measures the size of a star (Betelgeuse) | •U.S.: regular radio broadcasts begin | •Niels Bohr founds Physics Institute in Copenhagen | •First electric hair dryer |
| **1921** | •Chinese communist party founded | •Banting and Best discover insulin | •First use of the term robot, in a Karl Capek stage play | •Frederick Soddy: Nobel prize for isotope studies | •John Larson: polygraph, or lie detector |
| **1922** | •Russia becomes USSR | •Friedmann suggests that the Universe is expanding | •Refrigerators become common in U.S. | •John Plaskett discovers binary stars | •Choc-ice (Eskimo pies) |
| **1923** | •Italy: Mussolini seizes power | •BCG vaccine developed for tuberculosis (TB) | •Autogiro (early helicopter) flown in Spain | •Compton discovers the X-ray effect named after him | •Hot strip rolled steel process |
| **1924** | •Britain: first Labour government elected | •Edwin Hubble proves the existence of many galaxies | •U.S.: first Chrysler cars | •Oberath: The Rocket into Interplanetary Space | •Kleenex Celluwipes (first disposable paper tissues) |
| **1925** | •Albania gains independence •Iran: Reza Khan is shah | •Robert Millikan discovers cosmic rays | •Vladimir Zworykin: early type of TV set | •Karl Bosch invents process to make hydrogen gas | •Scotch tape •CinemaScope |
| **1926** | •Britain: General Strike | •Dangers of X rays identified | •J. L. Baird: first television | •Robert Goddard launches first liquid-fuel rocket | •First transistors |
| **1927** | •German stock market crash •Russia: Stalin vs. Trotsky | •Georges Lemaître suggests Big Bang theory | •First accelerators, or "atom-smashing" machines | •Werner Heisenberg: uncertainty principle | •First successful "talkie": The Jazz Singer |
| **1928** | •USSR: Stalin's first five-year plan | •Paul Dirac predicts the existence of antimatter | •Radio beacons for planes and ships | •Alexander Fleming discovers penicillin | •Quartz crystal clock |
| **1929** | •U.S.: Wall Street crash; Hoover elected president | •Matuyama describes Earth's magnetic field reversals | •Graf Zeppelin flies around the world in 27 days | •Van der Graaff: high-voltage "spark machines" | •Foam rubber (Dunlop Rubber Company) |
| **1930** | •India: Ghandi leads Salt March protest | •Tombaugh discovers Pluto, the last true planet | •First regular ship-to-shore radio-telephone messages | •Landsteiner: Nobel prize for blood group studies | •First sound recorder with magnetic tape |
| **1931** | •Japanese army occupies Chinese Manchuria | •Linus Pauling describes hybrid state of benzene | •UK: first outside TV broadcast (Derby horse race) | •Jansky: early studies on radio astronomy | •Jacob Schick: electric razor |
| **1932** | •Nazis take control of Reichstag (parliament) | •Positron and neutron atomic particles isolated | •First radio telescope | •Armand Quick: test to measure blood clotting | •Kodachrome color camera film |
| **1933** | •Hitler in power as Chancellor of Germany | •Tasmanian wolf becomes extinct | •Frequency modulation (FM) radio introduced | •Arthur Eddington: The Expanding Universe | •Polythene developed by ICI, a British chemical company |
| **1934** | •China: Mao Tse-tung leads communists on Long March | •First artificial radio-active element | •Beebe: dives to 3,280 feet (1,000 m) in bathysphere | •Beckman: pH meter to measure acids and alkalis | •Nylon •Cat's eye reflective road studs |
| **1935** | •Italy invades Abyssinia (Ethiopia) | •Turing describes computers in mathematical terms | •Germany: first TV broadcast station built | •Charles Richter: earthquake scale | •First beer cans •Technicolor for movies |
| **1936** | •Spanish Civil War begins •Edward VIII abdicates | •Oparin: "primeval soup" theory for the origin of life | •Volkswagen "Beetle" designed by Porsche | •Heinrich Focke: first practical helicopter | •Paperback books •Practical fluorescent lights |
| **1937** | •India: Congress Party wins elections | •First artificial element, technetium, created | •Whittle's first working jet engine | •Hans Krebs explains the body's cycle for using food | •Polyurethane chemicals |
| **1938** | •Germany and Austria unite (Anschluss) | •Hans Bethe describes the nuclear fusion of stars | •Teflon discovered | •Einstein and Infeld: The Evolution of Physics | •First ballpoint pens (biros) •First photocopiers tested |
| **1939** | •Spanish Civil War ends •World War II begins | •DDT used to kill malaria mosquitoes | •Heinkel builds first jet aircraft | •Lise Meitner introduces the term "nuclear fission" | •Sikorsky's helicopters go on sale |

# GLOSSARY

**anhydrous:** having no water.

**antimatter:** substances composed of atomic particles that have the same mass as an ordinary proton or electron, but have the opposite electrical charge. For example, a positron is the positive version of an ordinary electron, which has a negative charge.

**atom:** the smallest particle of a chemical element that can exist in nature either alone or combined with other elements.

**cryolite:** a soft, usually white mineral that is a compound of the elements aluminum, sodium, and flourine.

**electromagnetic energy:** a physical force generated by a combination of electric and magnetic fields, producing electromagnetic waves, such as visible and ultraviolet light rays, radio waves, microwaves, infrared waves, gamma rays, and X rays.

**element:** a pure, fundamental substance in nature, with atoms that are all exactly the same and which cannot be broken down by normal chemical methods into any other substances.

**glucagon:** a protein hormone that raises blood sugar by increasing the rate at which carbohydrates stored as glycogen in the liver are broken down.

**oxidant:** a substance that supplies the oxygen necessary for a fuel to burn.

**periodic table:** a chart of all the chemical elements arranged in horizontal rows, or periods, according to their atomic numbers, and in vertical groups of elements with similar properties and behaviors.

**polymer:** a chemical compound formed by combining molecules with duplicate structural units into larger molecules with the same proportion of elements but different physical properties.

# MORE BOOKS TO READ

*20s & 30s: Between the Wars. 20th Century Design* (series). Jackie Gaff (Gareth Stevens)

*The Boyhood Diary of Charles A. Lindbergh, 1913–1916: Early Adventures of the Famous Aviator.* Charles Lindbergh and Megan O'Hara (Blue Earth Books)

*The Empire State Building. Building America* (series). Craig A. Doherty and Katherine M. Doherty (Blackbirch)

*Great Discoveries & Inventions* (series). Antonio Casanellas (Gareth Stevens)

*Inside the Hindenburg.* Mireille Majoor (Little, Brown & Company)

*Just What the Doctor Ordered: The History of American Medicine. People's History* (series). Brandon Marie Miller (Lerner)

*Radio and Television. Communications Close-up* (series). Ian Graham (Raintree/Steck-Vaughn)

*Radio Astronomy. Above and Beyond* (series). Adele D. Richardson (Smart Apple Media)

*Rocket Man: The Story of Robert Goddard.* Thomas Streissguth (Carolrhoda Books)

# WEB SITES

Beetle Census: Beetle History. *www.beetlecensus.com/history.htm*

The Hindenburg. *www.pbs.org/wnet/secrets/html/e3-chemistry.html*

The Macrogalleria: a cyberwonderland of polymer fun. *www.psrc.usm.edu/macrog/*

MZTV Virtual Gallery: The Mechanical TV Era. *www.mztv.com/mech1.html*

Due to the dynamic nature of the Internet, some web sites stay current longer than others. To find additional web sites, use a reliable search engine with one or more of the following keywords: *atom smashing, autogiro, electron microscope, Edwin Hubble, Karl Jansky, jet engine, penicillin, periodic table, Pluto, steel,* and *Frank Whittle.*

# INDEX